AN OPEN AND NARRATED CITY	4
THE PROJECT	6
BELFAST- EAST BELFAST	9
LONDON- WHITECHAPEL	19
LJUBLJANA - CITY CENTER	29
ROMA - TRASTEVERE	45

UNA CITTÀ APERTA E RACCONTATA

La città e la sua architettura rappresentano fonti inesauribili di conoscenza, ispirazione e produzione. Sono contenitori e contenuti di forme, stili, progetti. Sono soggetti e oggetti. Nelle cavità e negli interstizi le persone si muovono e permangono, fuggono o visitano, ricercano o consolidano. In questi spazi concavi e convessi, in queste attività dicotomiche si svolge la vita del quotidiano: una vita quasi automatica, con una vista sulla città spesso astigmatica. Nasce quindi un desiderio, il più della volte inconsapevole, di spostare lo sguardo, di mettere a fuoco la città non vista, non percepita, non conosciuta, non vissuta. Un istinto che va oltre le pratiche quotidiane di riappropriazione dello spazio organizzato da parte dell'uomo, che *Michel De Certau* rintraccia e chiama *tattiche* (opposte alle strategie che invece indicano un luogo proprio). Queste infatti sono ingegnose operazioni quotidiane che mostrano una creatività incontrollata e una "stratificazione di funzionamenti diversi e interferenti". Ma quando invece la funzione è superata dalla specialità, quando l'oggetto diviene il soggetto, la città si descrive in prima persona: racconta la sua vita, ci mostra il suo corpo, le sue ambizioni e talvolta i suoi malanni.

Il desiderio di epifania della Città (nome proprio) è quello che la rete di *Open House Worldwide* (OHWW) raccoglie nel mondo. Non si guarda solo la funzionalità del corpo, ma ci si sofferma sulla bellezza delle membra e sulla grandezza del pensiero. Attraverso i progetti di Open House, promossi ad oggi in quasi 30 città di 4 continenti, la città per un weekend viene finalmente percepita nitidamente: la si può guardare da dentro, toccare, odorare, ascoltare.

L'ambizione di *Open City Roma* è infatti quella di creare una città aperta e raccontata. Si vuole mettere a fuoco lo sfondo. Uno sfondo fatto di documenti storici, di progetti architettonici, di cooperazione sociale e di produzione culturale.

Lo sguardo si posa sulle realtà urbane dimesse, sul dettaglio, sull'idea, sulla persona. Questa attenzione, questo spostamento tra figura e sfondo, questo desiderio di mostrare e di far apprezzare la città nella sua positiva complessità spingono il gruppo di Open City Roma a ricercare sentieri di esplorazione e comunicazione sempre diversi. Il progetto *Taste of a City* vuole leggere le particolarità di un quartiere rappresentativo delle città della rete OHWW attraverso l'unico senso mancante nell'apprezzamento della architettura e della vita che si svolge dentro e attorno: il gusto. Questa iniziativa editoriale nasce in occasione dell'Expo 2015 di Milano e sarà presentata negli spazi della Cascina Triulza, Padiglione della Società Civile, durante un calendario di eventi organizzati e promossi dalla Fondazione PLEF (Planet Life Economy Foundation).

Alessia Vitali

AN OPEN AND NARRETED CITY

The city and its architecture represent unlimited sources of knowledge, inspiration and production. They are containers and contents of forms, styles and projects. They are subjects and objects. In the crevices of the city, people move and linger, escape or visit, research or stabilize. Within these concave and convex spaces, within these contrasting activities, daily life moves on: a life almost automatic, with an often astigmatic view on the city. Therefore nearly an unconscious desire emerges: to shift the gaze and to focus the unseen, unperceived, unknown or unlived part of the city. An instinct emerges that goes beyond the everyday practices of repossessing the human organized space, what Michel De Certau traces and calls tattiche (strategies vs tactics). These are ingenious daily operations that show an uncontrolled creativity and a "stratification of different and interfering behaviors".

However, when, the specialty exceeds the function, when the object becomes the subjects, the city describes itself in first person: it tells its life, shows its body, its ambitions and sometimes its sickness.

The desire of the epiphany of the City (as a proper name) is what Open House Worldwide network (OHWW) gathers in the world, not only looking at the body functionality, but also at the beauty of the limbs and at the greatness of the thinking. Through the projects that Open House promotes in almost 30 cities in 4 continents, the city is finally seen clearly for a weekend: you can look at it from the inside, touch it, smell it and listen to it. Indeed, the ambition of Open City Roma is to create an open and narrated city. The aim is to focus on the background, a background made of historical document, architectural project, social cooperation and cultural production. The focus is on the disused urban realities, on the details, on the ideas and on the human being. This attention, this refocus on the figure and on the background, this desire to show the city and let it be appreciated in its positive complexity, drives the group of Open City Roma to constantly research new paths of exploration and communication.

The project "Taste of a City" wants to portray the characteristics of a representative neighborhood of the OHWW cities through taste, the only missing sense in the appreciation of architecture and of the life that is conducted all around it. This editorial initiative occurs in occasion of Expo Milano 2015, and will be presented in the space of Cascina Triulza-Civil Society Pavilion, during the events promoted and organized by PLEF (Planet Life Economy Foundation).

Alessia Vitali

IL PROGETTO

Se per un momento, fossimo in grado di immaginare e di assaggiare il sapore di un'architettura, di un quartiere o di una città?

Questo progetto è infatti alla ricerca di una degustazione che faccia cogliere la complessità e i contrasti di un ambiente urbano.

L'esperienza architettonica manca del solo gusto, siamo infatti soliti conoscerla con solo 4 sensi: il più immediato è sicuramente la vista, poi c'è il tatto, il più deciso, infine l'udito e l'olfatto, i più profondi.

Abbiamo chiesto alle città di *Open House Worldwide* (OHWW) di mettere in gioco un critico d'architettura e uno chef.

Il critico di architettura è stato invitato a scrivere un testo sensoriale che descrivesse uno dei quartieri più rappresentativi della sua città. Partendo quindi dalla selezione di una compagine urbana, i critici hanno descritto questi spazi attraverso odori, suoni, ricordi, metafore e percezioni organolettiche.

Lo chef è quindi stato invitato ad interpretare in note di gusto le aggettivazioni sensoriali del saggio, producendo una ricetta. Si era alla ricerca di una creazione culinaria che assorbisse nell'unico senso escluso dalla scoperta dell'architettura tutti gli altri quattro.

4 testi sensoriali e 4 ricette vi accompagneranno in questo primo viaggio di disvelamento dell'architettura attraverso il gusto.

Susan Berardo_studio laiBE

THE PROJECT

What if just for a moment we were able to imagine and to taste the flavor of an architecture, a neighborhood, or a city?

This project researches a tasting of the complexity, and the contrasts of an urban environment. The experience of architecture excludes only one sense: taste.

Indeed we usually appreciate architecture through four senses: the most immediate is certainly sight, then there is touch, the more decisive, and finally hearing and smell, certainly the most profound.

We invited the cities in the network of Open House Worldwide (OHWW) to put into play an architectural critic and a chef.

We asked the architecture critic to write a sensory text describing the most representative neighborhood of its city. Starting from an urban texture, the critic had to describe these spaces through smells, sounds, memories, metaphors and sensory perceptions.

We asked the chef to transcribe the sensory details of the essay in tasting notes, in a recipe. We are looking for a culinary creation capable of absorbing the four senses (sight, touch, hearing and smell) used to experience architecture in the only one excluded: taste.

4 sensory texts and 4 recipes will take you on this first trip of architecture disclosure through taste.

Susan Berardo_studio laiBE

THE VIEW FROM
MY WINDOW

I work in the former ***Strand Spinning Mill*** in East Belfast. It was built in the early 1900's. It was, for a time, the largest flax spinning mill in the world. Now, following a robust conversion, it houses design practices and a pottery, dance studios and a brewery. It rises amid the tiny terraced houses like a Gothic "cathederal" above the rooftops of a medieval town. It exudes the same confidence in engineered strucural masonry as does the cathederal and the same wanton disregard for the scale of its neighbours. However the houses and the factory share a common architectural aesthetic and materiality: rigorously repeated elegant arches executed in red brick, the same brick from which almost every pre-war building in

Belfast is built. These bricks were baked from clay excavated here in the city, they are now dull red with age, but were almost orange when new. On numerous of the terraced houses the red is (sometimes sparingly, sometimes downright flamboyantly) relieved in decorative detail executed in a yellow brick derived from an alien clay. From my window I look back across East Belfast towards the city centre.

East Belfast is (or more properly, was) the home to numerous industrial superlatives: for half a century or more, in this part of this city, they built the world's biggest ships and spun the worlds longest ropes; they wove the world's finest linen and managed to sustain one of the world's most intractable internecine conflicts. It is both the birth place of Belfast's most famous poet, *Van Morrison*, and it offers the subject matter for many of his lyrics. Sloth, or inertia, are the lesser of my motivations in choosing this view about which to write: not to have to leave my desk in search of inspiration is indeed convenient but in truth this view encompasses almost all of those phenomena which, in combination, uniquely define East Belfast's urban character.

From my privileged first floor office I look northwest towards the city centre across rows of tiny terraced houses, saw-tooth, north lit factory roofs, towards the shipyards and the docks. The view is ultimately contained (like the city itself) by the profile of the handsome *Cave Hill* and its lumpen neighbours the *Black Mountain and Divis*. In late spring and summer these "Belfast Hills" which for the rest of the year exhibit dull earthy tones light up with yellow gorse no less vibrant than the huge cranes of the ship yard which dominate the middle distance. The spiky outlines of the oilrigs under repair in the otherwise now obsolete yards glow like Christmas trees at night. The view is punctuated with the polychrome splashes of the partisan flags which still mark out the sectarian territories of this city no less emphatically than dog piss on a lamp post. Neither the country side nor the sea is far away: the screaming seagulls (competing with screaming Airbuses, descending rakishly into "City Airport") remind us of the proximity of Belfast Lough. On still summer evenings the acrid smell of smoke from gorse fires in the nearby hills (casually lit by Belfast kids for their personal diversion) drifts into the narrow *Victorian streets* and even the sweetly rancid stench of manure from the fields beyond the suburbs occassionally mingles with the smoke from coal fires and the alluring scent of deep fat frying from the numerous fish and chip shops along the main thoroughfares. Most of what was once great about the urban fabric of East Belfast is now in decay, Stand Mill is an exception.

The straight narrow streets, built to house the rural masses who rushed into Belfast in the second half of the nineteenth century (as fodder for Imperial Industry), are being demolished in favour of private and social housing, more self-consciously designed, but exhibiting a bland, miss-placed suburban quality. The massively interesting and physically huge "*World's Largest Ropeworks*" in the heart of the area is gone and in its place a sprawling mess of tin sheds housing American fast food outlets and German grocers. They are set randomly among hectares of carparking with no regard for history or respect for continuity.

We should at least be grateful that the memory of East Belfast as a characterful, unique urban place is preserved in the lyrics of Van Morrison's songs, such as these from his autobiographical:

CLEANING WINDOWS

"OH, THE SMELL OF THE BAKERY FROM ACROSS THE STREET GOT IN MY NOSE...
WE WENT FOR LEMONADE AND PARIS BUNS AT THE SHOP AND BROKE FOR TEA"

THE AUTHOR

Aidan McGrath

Born and raised in Belfast, he was educated at Queens University Belfast.
He is Member of the Royal Institute of British Architects and the Architects Registration Board (of the United Kingdom), Founding Director of *Twenty Two Over Seven Architects*, partner in McGonigle McGrath architects and judge in a number of National and International Design Competitions (including The Giant's Causeway Visitor Centre and the West Belfast Expo). Former Acting Excecutive Director of PLACE, the Architecture Centre in Belfast, he contributes to architectural press (including AJ, Beaumeister and Perspective magazines). His interests beyond architecture include photography and "food" both of which feed directly his third love: travel.
He has a particular fondness for Italy (Umbria, Marche and Emilia-Romagna in particular) and the wildernesses of western USA including Alaska.

THE CHEF

Niall McKenna is a son of Belfast. He spent his formative years working in the city with some of Ireland's finest chefs before, in 1994, moving to London to garner further invaluable experience in the kitchens of the capital's best restaurants.

He returned to Belfast in 2000 and began to grow his culinary empire. He began with the fine dining establishment ***James Street South***.

He now has four restaurants, all in his native city. The fifth, which will occupy a former Victorian sail loft on a city quay, is currently planned. Traditionally Belfast enjoyed a huge range of fresh breads and sweet pastries. For many years, life in the narrow terrace streets was enriched by the arrival of tiny, humming, electric vans: *the bread man cometh*.

The rear doors opened and the driver pulled out 3 meter long wooden drawers brimming with a huge variety of breads: *pan loaf and plain; Belfast baps and barmbrac; wheaten bread, soda farls and treacle loaf, not to mention milk scone and the near mystical malty "Veda"*.

Life for the family was indeed good when the housewife purchased not just her daily fresh crusty bread but sweet cakes: *Paris buns or snowballs, iced fingers or gravy rings, custards and German biscuits*. In difference to this tradition Chef Niall McKenna has chosen a bread recipe to typify Belfast cuisine. Specifically wheaten bread, for which there is a long tradition throughout not just this city but all of Ireland. Niall raises it from the everyday with the addition of "dulce butter" and smoked salmon. Both the dulce (an edible seaweed) and the smoked salmon evoke the city's maritime connections.

NIALL MCKENNA

James Street South and The Bar and Grill at James Street South
21 James Street South, Belfast, BT2 7GA

Hadski's
Commercial Court, Belfast BT1 2NB

Cast and Crew
Queen's Road, Titanic Quarter, Belfast

IRISH WHEATEN BREAD WITH
SEAWEED BUTTER AND SMOKED SALMON

WHEATEN BREAD
Makes 2 loaves
750 g T55 (bread flour)
375 g wholemeal flour
2 teaspoons of salt
1 litre buttermilk
2 teaspoons bicarbonate of soda
1 tablespoon honey

SEAWEED BUTTER
50 g butter
2 teaspoons of dill
20 g dulse (edible seaweed)
2 button shallots
1 lemon juiced
10 g capers
2 cloves garlic

GARNISH
5 g dill
5 g chervil
5 g shiso

Mix all dry ingredients together in bowl. Add buttermilk and beat for 2 minutes until the mix forms a dough. Mould into a flat circle and cut a cross into the top.

Place on a baking tray and cook at 170°C in combination oven for 40 minutes.
To make sure it is cooked the full way through you can use a knitting needle to do this, if it comes out clean take out of oven.

To make the butter take 10g butter in warm pan and melt and sweat the finely chopped shallots, chopped garlic for 3 mins.

In a bowl place the capers, half of the lemon juice, finely chopped dulse, dill and cooled shallots. Mix with the remaining butter which should be at room temperature. Season with a pinch of salt and pepper and place in fridge.

WHITECHAPEL

There is nowhere that better symbolizes London in all its electrifying glory than **Whitechapel**. This tangle of crowded streets just to the east of the City is far from perfect, of course. Most of its post-war buildings are downright ugly, it has pockets of extreme poverty (alongside enclaves of great wealth), and it is relentlessly urban.

Its charm is in the way that over half a millennia it has managed to combine the most unlikely elements, producing streets where a fine Georgian terrace neighbours a 1970s block of social housing, a skyline where a mosque's minaret is cheek by jowl with a steel and glass skyscraper and where, walking past a tattoo parlour, it is possible to observe the ghost of a sign advertising the services of a long-dead tailor painted into the brickwork of the building.

Whitechapel is like Van Gogh painting in the garden Saint-Paul Asylum, the institution

Images of 19th Century

where he was treated before his death: vivid, gorgeous, unsettling and frenetic.

Its urban story begins in the 16th century when it developed as an industrial estate serving the City of London. Tanneries, breweries, slaughterhouses and metal foundries were set up and, amidst these noxious trades, lived impoverished workers and their families.

This is where Joseph Merrick, the *Elephant Man*, was exhibited in a shop before coming to the attention of Dr Frederick Treves, who worked across the road at the Royal London Hospital.

It is also where the notorious serial killer *Jack the Ripper* killed at least five of the area's many prostitutes during 1888. Whitechapel was London's first slum, and it is said that *Charles Dickens* based Fagin in Oliver Twist on a famous 19th century "fence" (receiver of stolen goods) who operated in the area.

It is hard not to be affected by these stories; one of the most evocative corners of Whitechapel remains *Cable Street* where, in 1936, thousands of mainly poor Jewish protesters converged to prevent the jackbooted British Union of Fascists marching through their streets using home-made barricades.

The area's Jewish community is just one demographic layer in an area which has provided a home for refugees from near (Ireland) and far (Bangladesh).

Whilst not cohesive, in terms of individual buildings Whitechapel has some absolute jewels. *Wilton's Music Hall* is one of the last surviving music halls in the world, the original building dating from the 1690s. A recent, sensitive restoration has preserved its sense of peeling grandeur, its proscenium arch-stage is a fading beauty.

Another favourite is the Whitechapel Gallery, with its original tiled façade and a well-judged more recent addition - a roof top weather vane by the artist *Rodney Graham* the 16th century scholar Erasmus riding a horse backwards while engrossed in the pages of a book.

The building was once *Whitechapel Library* which has now moved to new premises designed by *David Adjaye* in panes of transparent and colored glass mimicking the stripes of vendors' stalls in the historic *Whitechapel Market*. The 21st century is bringing yet more change to Whitechapel. Savills estate agents reports that its combination of centrality and relative affordability means it has quietly become London's number one location for affluent under 35s.

Developers are responding, most notably at Goodman's Fields a seven-acre mixed-use scheme, designed by *Lifschutz Davidson Sandilands* for Berkeley Homes on land where food was once grown for a mediaeval nunnery. This 900-home scheme will, no doubt, bring a slew of organic delis and nail bars to Whitechapel, adding yet another layer to the story of this great survivor.

THE AUTHOR

Ruth Bloomfield

Ruth Bloomfield is an award-winning property and architecture writer, who contributes to newspapers including the London Evening Standard, Times, Sunday Times, and Wall Street Journal. As a former news editor of both the Evening Standard and London's Time Out Magazine she has been covering news in the British capital for more than a decade.

THE CHEF

Cecily Darling

Cecily Darling is a 25 year old chef from London. She has worked under *Theo Randall and Rowley Leigh*, and is currently at *The River Café* in London where she has been delighting in the culinary traditions of Italy. Cecily has lived the vast majority of her life in London, and has come to know many of its neighbourhoods intimately. She thoroughly enjoys the wide variety of characters and flavours in each, all the while feeling at home surrounded by the schizophrenic combination of its mongrel architecture.

The River Cafè
Thames Wharf
Rainville Rd
London W6 9HA

JUNIPER MARINATED MACKEREL
WITH FENNEL AND CUCUMBER

TO SERVE 2 AS A MAIN OR 4 AS A STARTER

FOR THE MARINADE

12 juniper berries, gently crushed
1 bay leaf
2 cloves garlic, gently crushed
10 whole peppercorns
400 ml cold water
100 g caster sugar
150 ml lemon juice

4 mackerel fillets, pin-boned
1 bulb fennel
1 cucumber
chili flakes (optional)
Olive oil, red wine vinegar, salt and pepper to dress

Combine all ingredients for the marinade, except sugar and lemon, and bring to the boil. Once boiled, turn down heat and simmer for two minutes. Turn off the heat, add sugar and lemon juice and allow to cool.
Arrange mackerel fillets skin side up in a shallow dish so that they are not overlapping. Pour over the marinade, ensuring the mackerel is just submerged - reserve some marinade and reduce until slightly thicker for a sauce. Cover the mackerel and leave for at least 2 hours somewhere cool.
Meanwhile, cut the cucumber into long even strips using a peeler. Salt the cucumber gently and leave in a sieve over a bowl so that the liquid drains off. Slice the fennel as thinly as possible using a sharp knife or a mandolin. Store in iced water to prevent discoloring and to keep it crisp.
Just before serving, combine the dried fennel and squeezed cucumber strips and dress gently with olive oil and red wine vinegar, salt, pepper and a few chili flakes (if using). Remove the mackerel from the marinade and pat dry (discard the fishy marinade). Season on both sides with salt and pepper. Heat a heavy, preferably non-stick frying pan until extremely hot. Add just a small amount of flavorless oil (sunflower or vegetable) to coat the bottom of the pan. The oil should be almost smoking before laying the mackerel skin side down in the pan. Hold down the fillet to prevent them from curling up before adding the next. Give the pan a small shake to prevent the fish from sticking. After just a minute (depending on size of fillets) flip them over to cook on the flesh side for just a few seconds. The skin should have some colour and crisp, but not be burnt.
Serve immediately with your freshly combined crunchy salad and the warm, reduced juniper marinade.

WHAT DO YOU THINK LJUBLJANA CITY CENTER

IS MADE OF?

IZ ČESA JE NAREJENA LJUBLJANA?

Love for our past and dreams for our future prevent us from looking at our present.
The capital city of Slovenia is LJUBLJANA. For foreigners is very difficult to pronounce but in fact it is very simple. You just need to know that it means «the loved one».
LJUBLJANA city center was carefully constructed with LOVE and is constantly changing by LOVE.

LOVE as imagination and desire for knowledge.
LOVE as the means of change.
LOVE as the creative potential of individuals.

Ljubljana city center is not an ideal center. It is just a common place like many others in the world. But is real and has a long memory.
Ljubljana city center was grown in «liliput» scale, many tiny streets, pedestrians avenues, cyclic lanes, romantic atmosphere and white castle above the city centre. Ljubljana city center has a river that slowly flows through the city and open another dimension of living in the capital.
Ljubljana city center connects people. Bridges expanding across the river represent the invisible touch of contradictions.
Ljubljana city center believes in space rather than time. People in space create places.
And Ljubljana city center is a special place. It is old but is constantly refreshed.

Ljubljana city center has a lot of trees. Old big chestnuts with wide green shadows.

Ljubezen do preteklosti in sanje o prihodnosti nam zastirajo pogled na sedanjost.
Ljubljana je glavno mesto Slovenije. Tujci njeno ime težko izgovorijo, vendar je v svojem bistvu precej enostavno. Vedeti je potrebno le, da pomeni «ljubljena».
Središče LJUBLJANE je bilo subtilno sestavljeno z LJUBEZNIJO in se stalno spreminja z LJUBEZNIJO.

LJUBEZEN, ki jo razumemo kot sanje in hrepenenje po znanju.
LJUBEZEN, ki spodbuja spremembe.
LJUBEZEN, kot ustvarjalni potencial posameznikov.

Središče Ljubljane ni idealno mesto. Predstavlja skupni prostor meščanov, kot številni po svetu.
A hkrati je prostor sedanjosti, z zelo dolgo in bogato zgodovino.
Ljubljansko središče ima človeku prijazne razdalje, ozke ulice, varne pešpoti, urejene kolesarske steze, romantične kotičke in bel grad nad mestom.
Skozi mesto počasi polzi reka Ljubljanica, ki mestni sliki dodaja nove dimenzije.
Središče Ljubljane povezuje ljudi. Mostovi, ki se pnejo iz levega na desni breg predstavljajo nevidni stik nasprotij.

Središče Ljubljane se bolj kot v času, zrcali v prostoru. Ljudje v njem ustvarjajo posebna mesta.
In središče Ljubljane je res posebno, je staro, a hkrati sveže.
Središče Ljubljane ima veliko dreves. Stari kostanji v njem oblikujejo prostrane zelene sence.

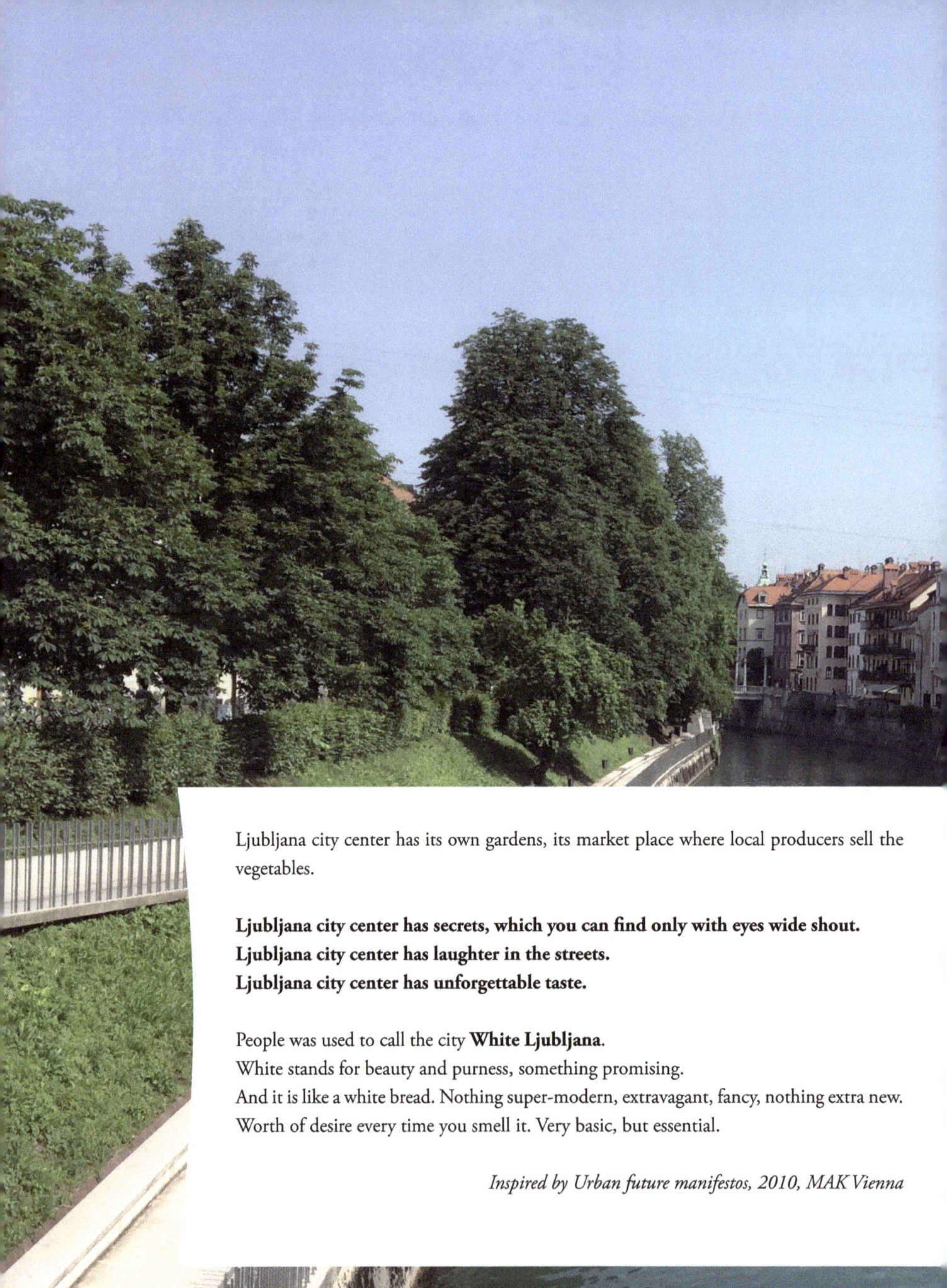

Ljubljana city center has its own gardens, its market place where local producers sell the vegetables.

Ljubljana city center has secrets, which you can find only with eyes wide shout.
Ljubljana city center has laughter in the streets.
Ljubljana city center has unforgettable taste.

People was used to call the city **White Ljubljana**.
White stands for beauty and purness, something promising.
And it is like a white bread. Nothing super-modern, extravagant, fancy, nothing extra new.
Worth of desire every time you smell it. Very basic, but essential.

Inspired by Urban future manifestos, 2010, MAK Vienna

Središče Ljubljane ima svoje vrtove, svoj trg, kjer lokalni proizvajalci prodajajo domačo zelenjavo.

Središče Ljubljane ima svoje skrivnosti, ki jih lahko najdeš le z s pozornim očesom.
Središče Ljubljane ima smeh na ulicah.
Središče Ljubljane ima nepozabni okus.

Ljudje so nekdaj Ljubljano imenovali **Bela Ljubljana**.
Bela kot lepa, čista, ki kot nevesta ženina, zapelje svoje prebivalce.
In bela kot kruh. Nič posebnega, ekstravagantnega, trendovskega, nič novega. Vredna poželjenja, vsakič znova, ko jo povonjaš. Zelo enostavna, a hkrati bistvena.

Navdih po Urban future manifestos, 2010, MAK Dunaj

THE AUTHORS

Ana Struna Bregar & Lenka Kavčič

Lenka Kavčič (1968) and **Ana Struna Bregar** (1975) are both architects, critics and event managers.
Lenka Kavčič was vice dean of the Faculty of Design in Ljubljana between the 2009 and 2013. Ana Struna Bregar was director of House of Architecture by the Chamber of Architecture and Spatial Planning of Slovenia between 2009 and 2013.

In 2013 they founded a private institute Afront (which means: good ideas have to go and front of the others), through which they organize several different projects. They run the biggest slovene architectural festival *Open House Slovenia*.
With the communication, promotion and organization of events their institution encourages investors and customers to use excellent sustainable architectural solutions. In 2012, the Open House Slovenia project got the highest slovene architectural award plecnik's medal.
In 2013, they got the same *Plecnik's medal* also for educating children about architecture - for the project playful architecture.
In 2015, they made the interior design for the first slovene puppet museum in Ljubljana.

THE CHEF

Klemen Košir

Klemen Košir (1974) is an independent publicist whose main interest for the last decade has been on eating culture. The centre of his attention is man with all his needs, imperfections, past and wishes captured in space and time. For Klemen, food serves as an excuse to go on a field trip to knock on farmers' or wine growers' door, to stop in a remote village and join a crowd of local people or simply to enjoy a chat with a fisherman on the coast. He finds that writing and publishing books is the karma he is happy to embrace.

My Daily Bread is Košir's third book, coming out after his well-received Namazi Za Mizo (Table Spreads, 2012) and FAO 37.2.1 - the Wild Adriatic (2013), winner of multiple awards.

His book on bread won the *Most Beautiful Slovenian Book Award* at the Slovenian Book Fair 2014. Graphic design by Kabinet01.

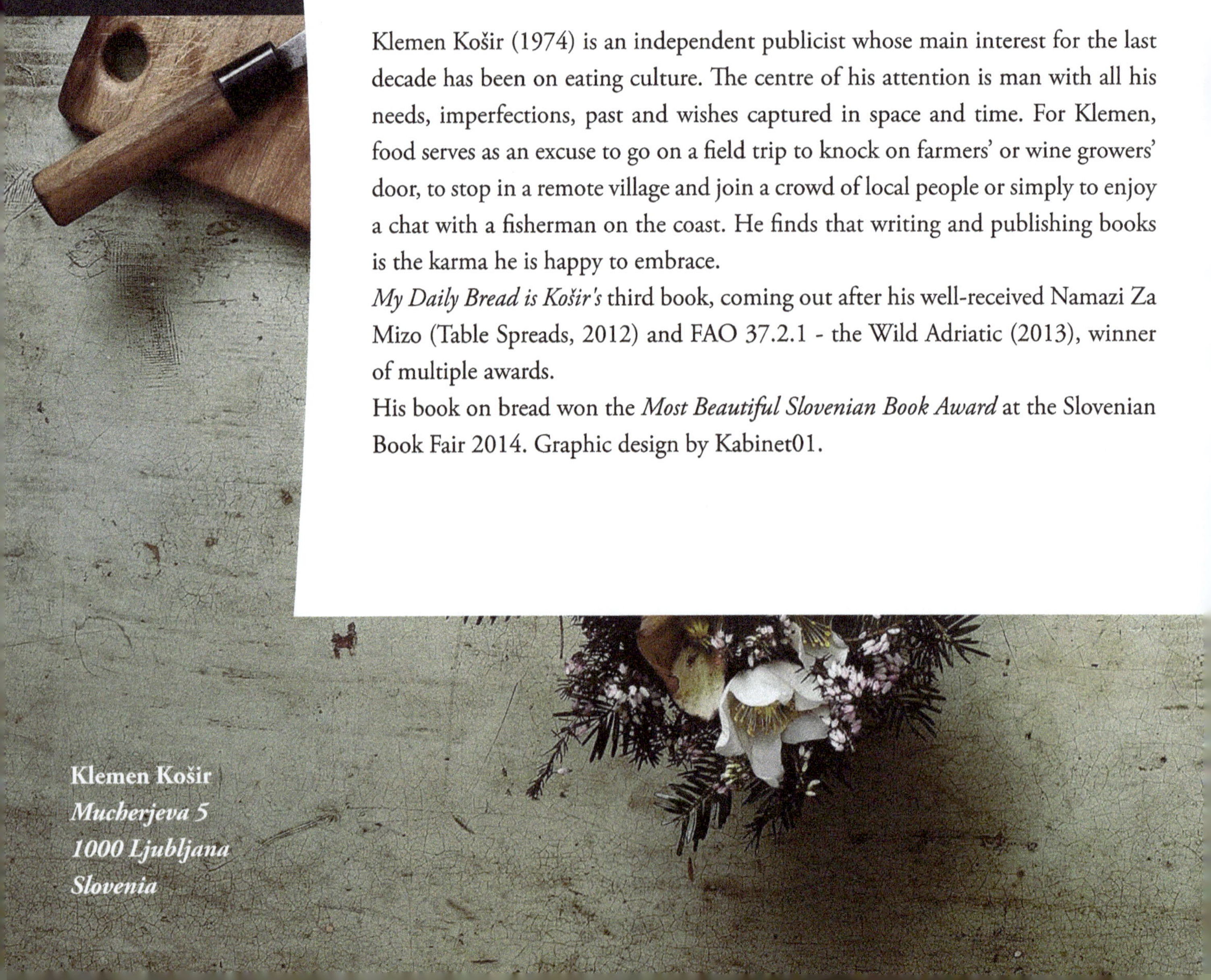

Klemen Košir
Mucherjeva 5
1000 Ljubljana
Slovenia

MY HEART BEATS FOR RYE BREAD

It's so fragrant, with full, sweet and sour flavour and a moist crumb. It goes with practically everything and everyone, so it just calls for socializing and company of other dishes. High in pentosans that, together with fiber, absorb water like a sponge, it stays fresh for up to a week, which makes for a genuine ecological statement. And it's modest - rye flour usually sits on the lowest shelf in the store and costs only a third of the price you would pay for the popular and trendy spelt flour. Should I ever have to reach for only one type of bread to chew on for the rest of my days, it would be rye. O'Ryelly takes a step forward, incorporating wholegrain wheat flour and kefir into a wholesome and tasty compromise.

Srce mi bije za kruh iz ržene moke, tako dehteč je, polnega, sladko-kislega okusa in sočne sredice. Poda se k praktično vsem jedem in ni prav nič zahteven za druženje in kombiniranje. Zaradi pentosanov, ki skupaj z vlakninami kot goba vsrkajo vodo, ohranja svežino tudi do teden dni, kar je čisti ekološki statement. In še skromnega značaja je - ržena moka običajno ždi na najnižji polici trgovine, cena za kilogram je trikrat nižja kot za popularno in trendovsko pirino moko. Če bi že moral poseči po le eni vrsti kruha, ki bi ga žvečil do konca življenja, bi bil le ta rženi. Ržo gre korak naprej in je s kombiniranjem polnozrnate pšenične moke in dodatkom kefirja zdrav in okusen kompromis.

THE RECIPE

O' RYELLY: AROMATIC ROUND RYE LOAF WITH KEFIR STARTER

ONE ROUND LOAF
SPONGE
500 g wholegrain rye flour
300 g wholegrain wheat flour
500 ml full-fat kefir
(can be replaced with an equal amount of water)
300 ml cold water
5 g fresh yeast

FINAL DOUGH
Mature Sponge
200 g wholegrain rye flour
18 g sea salt

100 g strong wheat flour for handling and dusting
a handful of rye, wheat or spelt bran for the base

Equipment Rectangular sheet pan

Sponge Pour the kefir into a large bowl. Dissolve the yeast in cold water and add the mixture to the kefir. With a wooden spoon stir the liquid and gradually add flour, starting with rye and finishing with wheat flour. Stir until you have a thin, homogenous, lump-free mixture. Cover the bowl with a wet tea towel and leave the sponge to mature at room temperature overnight or about eight hours. This will allow the sponge to bubble and slightly swell.

Kneading Salt the mature sponge and thicken with the remaining rye flour. Stir with a wooden spoon until the flour has absorbed all the liquid and you get a sticky, dense mixture.

Maturation Cover the dough with a wet tea towel and leave to rest for 20 minutes. Stir again quickly, cover with the towel and leave to rest for another 20 minutes.

Shaping Dust the work surface with strong flour and transfer the dough from the bowl. Now dust the surface of the dough as well and then quickly, but firmly, knead it by folding the edges, one after another, towards the centre. Dust with more flour, if it's too sticky. You now have a round loaf.
Sprinkle the bottom of a sheet pan with bran and place the loaf with the rough side down to hide the folds. Dust the surface of the loaf with flour and press it

AROMATIČNI RŽENI HLEB S KEFIRJEVIM NASTAVKOM

1 HLEBEC

PREDTESTO
50 dag polnozrnate ržene moke
30 dag polnozrnate pšenične moke
5 dl polnomastnega kefirja (lahko ga nadomestimo z enako količino vode)
3 dl hladne vode
5 g svežega kvasa

KONČNO TESTO
zorjeno predtesto
20 dag polnozrnate ržene moke
18 g morske soli

10 dag ostre pšenične moke za rokovanje in posip
pest rženih, pšeničnih ali pirinih otrobov za podlago

Pravokoten *pekač z nizkim robom*

Predtesto *Polnomasten kefir zlijemo v večjo skledo. Dolijemo hladno vodo, v kateri smo raztopili sveži kvas. S kuhalnico mešamo tekočino in postopoma dodajamo moko, najprej rženo, nato pšenično. Mešamo toliko časa, dokler ne dobimo redke homogene zmesi brez grudic. Skledo prekrijemo z mokro kuhinjo krpo in pustimo predtesto zoreti na sobni temperaturi čez noč oziroma 8 ur.*

Zamesitev *Zorjeno predtesto solimo in ga zgostimo s preostankom ržene moke. Testo mešamo s kuhalnico toliko časa, dokler vsa moka ne vpije tekočine. Dobili bomo lepljivo kompaktno zmes.*

Zorenje *Testo prekrijemo z mokro krpo in ga pustimo počivati 20 minut. Nato ga še enkrat na hitrico premešamo, prekrijemo s krpo in pustimo počivati nadaljnjih 20 minut.*

Oblikovanje *Z ostro pšenično moko posujemo delovno površino in nanj preložimo testo. Moko posujemo še po površini testa, nato ga z odločnimi gibi na hitro pregnetemo tako, da ga krog in krog prepogibamo od zunanjega roba proti sredini mase. Delamo hitro in odločno. Če je testo preveč lepljivo, ga dodatno posujemo z moko. Dobili bomo okrogel hlebec.*
Dno nizkega pekača posujemo z otrobi in nanj položimo hlebec testa z grobim delom, kjer so gube ob prepogibanja, obrnjenim navzdol.

down with the heel of your hand to flatten it out a little. With your fingers and the palm of your hand gently massage the surface of the dough with circular movements, rubbing the flour into the surface to smoothen it out and flatten out the loaf a little more. Sprinkle with more flour if necessary as you need friction between your hand and the dough.

Proofing Cover the dough with a tea towel and leave to mature for about two hours. This is the time for fermentation to take place, gases will be released and the top of the dough will start to rise and crack, giving the bread its distinctive appearance. Half an hour before you stop proofing, pre-heat the oven to 240 °C and place the rack at the bottom of the oven.

Baking Before baking, dust the proofed cracked loaf with strong flour and place the pan with the loaf into the pre-heated oven. Bake at high temperature for the first six minutes then lower to 220 °C and bake for another 40 to 45 minutes, depending on how thick your loaf is. Take the baked bread out of the oven and transfer it to a wire rack or somewhere with good air circulation and leave to cool for at least two hours or, even better, overnight.

Tip Kefir is used in baking for its high content of milk bacteria. When you knead dough with kefir culture you accelerate the development of bacteria that endow bread with its pleasant flavour and aroma. While fats give kefir bread a softer taste and denser structure, they also make the bread dry more quickly and reduce its shelf life. To extend your bread's shelf life you can leave out kefir and replace it with the same amount of water.

KNEADING THE SPONGE
10 minutes

SPONGE MATURATION
8 hours

KNEADING THE DOUGH
10 minutes, 20 minutes to rest + 20 minutes to rest

DOUGH MATURATION
2 hours

SHAPING THE LOAF
15 minutes

PROOFING
2 hours

BAKING
first 6 minutes at 240 °C + 40 to 45 minutes at 220 °C, bottom oven rack

COOLING
2 hours, preferably

Pomokamo površino hlebca in ga s spodnjim delom dlani večkrat pritisnemo navzdol, da se nekoliko splošči in razširi. S prsti in dlanjo začnemo površino nežno krožno masirati po celotni površini. S tem vtiramo moko v povrhnjico in jo gladimo, obenem pa hlebec še nekoliko sploščimo. Po potrebi dodatno posujemo hlebec z moko, ker mora biti med dlanjo in testom trenje.

Vzhajanje Testo prekrijemo s kuhinjsko krpo in ga pustimo zoreti približno 2 uri. V tem času bo potekala fermentacija, sproščali se bodo plini in povrhnjica testa bo začela nabrekati in pokati. Prav razpoke so prepoznavni znak rženega kruha. Proti koncu vzhajanja segrejemo pečico na 240 °C, rešetke postavimo na spodnji nivo.

Peka Vzhajani razpokani hlebec pred peko še enkrat posujemo z ostro pšenično moko, nato ga s pekačem vred postavimo v segreto pečico. Prvih 6 minut pečemo pri visoki temperaturi, nato jo znižamo na 220 °C in hlebec pečemo še 40 do 45 minut, odvisno od debeline.
Pečen kruh vzamemo iz pečice in ga prestavimo na zračno površino, kjer se naj ohlaja vsaj 2 uri, še raje čez noč.

Nasvet Kefir se v pekarstvu uporablja zaradi visokega deleža mlečnih bakterij. Ko zamesimo testo s kefirjevo kulturo, pospešimo razvoj bakterij, ki pridajo kruhu prijetno aromo in okus. Kefirjev kruh bo zaradi maščob mehkejšega okusa in gostejše strukture, iz istega razloga pa se bo prej posušil oziroma imel krajšo življenjsko dobo. Za daljšo obstojnost kruha lahko kefir izpustimo in ga nadomestimo z vodo v enakem razmerju.

TRASTEVERE
THE HYPERPRESEPIO

Trastevere sta al centro storico di Roma come il Village sta a Manhattan. È il luogo in cui si rappresenta l'antica storia della città, il suo presepio. Ma poiché, a sua volta, il centro storico di Roma è il presepio dell'intera area metropolitana di Roma, Trastevere ne è il presepio al quadrato, l'hyperpresepio. Nel presepio ci sono le montagne di cartapesta, il fiume, la caserma e i pastorelli. A Trastevere la collina è il Gianicolo, il fiume è il Tevere e poi c'è il carcere di Regina Coeli con Erode e il mercato di Porta Portese. È più difficile trovare Gesù, la Madonna e San Giuseppe. Secondo me potrebbero ben stare nella Chiesa di Santa Maria in Trastevere che è il cuore del quartiere.
Come tutti i presepi, Trastevere è allo stesso momento vero e finto: l'apoteosi del simile e del

Trastevere relates to the historical center of Rome as the Village to Manhattan. It's the "presepio" (nativity scene) of the city, where the ancient history is performed. But since, in turn, the historic center of Rome is the "presepio" of the entire metropolitan area, Trastevere is its "presepio" to the square, the hyperpresepio.
In the "presepio" there are papier-mache mountains, a river, a station and shepherds.
In Trastevere the Gianicolo is the hill, the Tiber is the river, and then there is the prison of Regina Coeli with Herod and the market of Porta Portese. It's harder to find Jesus, Mary and Joseph. In my opinion, they might well be in the Church of Santa Maria in Trastevere which is the heart of the neighborhood.

verosimile. È una realtà stratificata con preziosi reperti storici, ma è anche una ricostruzione fasulla della storia rifatta ad uso e consumo dei turisti, per i quali non è così importante aggirarsi tra ciò che ha duemila anni di storia o ciò che è stato velocemente invecchiato. Il motore trainante è il turismo che lo usa come presepe abitabile. Credo che sia il luogo più identitario della romanità e insieme con il maggior numero di stranieri residenti e con la maggiore densità di strutture ricettive. Naturalmente tracima di bar e ristoranti. La gran parte dei quali trasmette il suo inconfondibile odore: a metà tra il buon sapore di cucinato e la puzza di bollito e di fritto. Un odore che si scontra con quello di umido delle chiese.

La regola del presepe è che la storia non è mai tragica: le catapecchie non crollano, l'acqua non produce allagamenti, la paglia non va a fuoco, il freddo è sempre sopportabile. È la strategia del pittoresco dove tutto è vecchio e funzionante allo stesso tempo. Un micro-universo disordinato ma dove il disordine è la via di fuga all'ordine di un mondo sempre più perfetto e inumano. Dove si respira aria di uguaglianza tra il pastorello e il re dei Magi. Dove i buoni sentimenti fanno spazio alle ambizioni.

Dicevo che, affinché il verosimile sia tale, serve che sia radicato nel vero. Trastevere ne ospita numerosi lacerti. Tra gli infiniti turisti si trovano ancora i romani di Roma, tra le nuove strutture commerciali le antiche. E poi vi sono le chiese. Una più bella dell'altra, una più remota dell'altra. La mia sensazione è che rappresentino delle macchine del tempo che permettono all'hyper-presepe di avvicinarsi alla dimensione mistica. Perché tutti i presepi sono uguali ma ciascuno deve essere a suo modo unico. E forse l'unicità di Trastevere è che è uno dei pochi quartieri di Roma dove ancora il Medioevo con la sua pervasiva religiosità comanda.

Like all the "presepi", Trastevere is at the same time real and fake: the apotheosis of similar and likely.

It's a reality layered with precious historical artifacts, but is also a fake reconstruction of history, remade for the consumption of tourists, for whom it is not so important to be somewhere between what has two thousand years of history or what was aged quickly.

The driving force is tourism that uses it as a livable "presepio". I think it's the place where you can find the most of the Roman identity together with the largest number of foreign residents and with the highest density of accommodation. It includes an overflow of bars and restaurants, with their unique smell: something between the good taste of food and the stink of boiled and fried. A smell that collides with the humid odor of the churches. The principle of the "presepio" is that history is never tragic: slums don't collapse, rivers don't overflow, straw doesn't catch on fire and cold is always bearable. It's the strategy of picturesque, where everything is old and at the same time perfectly functioning. A messy micro-universe where disorder is the way out from an orderly world more and more perfect and inhuman. Where the shepherd and the king of the Magi are equal. Where good feelings make room for ambitions. As I said, in order to have verisimilitude, you need to be rooted in what is truly real. In Trastevere there are many fragments. Among the countless tourists you can still find the true Romans, as among the new shops you can still find the traditional ones. And then, there are the churches. Each one more beautiful than the other, each one more remote than the other. My feeling is that they represent the time machines that allow the hyperpresepio to reach the mystical dimension.

All the "presepi" are the same, but each one has to be in its way unique. Perhaps the uniqueness of Trastevere is that it's one of the few neighborhoods in Rome where the Middle Ages still dominates with its pervasive religiosity.

LUIGI PRESTINENZA PUGLISI

Luigi Prestinenza Puglisi is an architectural writer, critic and the president of **Associazione Italiana di Architettura e Critica** *(www.architetturaecritica.com)*. He is the director of the weekly **presS/Tletter** *(www.presstletter.com)*, a newsletter born in 2003 when he has understood the potentiality of this vehicle for Italian architecture community. His many books include: *HyperArchitecture, Birkhäuser and New Directions in Contemporary Architecture. Evolutions and Revolutions in Building Design Since 1988, Wiley.* His pages on social network are another instrument to propose a never finished critic of architecture.

Most of his books, as History of Contemporary Architecture 1976-2001, are free downloadable on website www.prestinenza.it, where he continuously publishes chronicles, comments, portraits about architects and architecture.

THE AUTHOR

Glass Hostaria
Vicolo del Cinque 58, Roma
www.glasshostaria.it

Romeo Chef&Baker
Via Silla 26a, Roma
www.romeo.roma.it

THE CHEF

CRISTINA BOWERMAN

After graduating in Law, Cristina Bowerman continued her studies in Forensics at the University of San Francisco in California. Ten years later, she gained a degree in *Culinary Arts* in 2002 at the University of Austin, TX (Cordon Bleu).

In 2004, she decided to return to Italy for a short period of time to work at *Convivio Troiani*. At the end of 2005, she was offered the direction of *Glass Hostaria* with Fabio Spada and Silvia Sacerdoti. In 2009, Cristina received a *Michelin Star*, the only woman for that year.

She was nominated Chef of the Year in 2013 by *Identità Golose*. Cristina continues to cultivate her passion and is always studying the application of science in the kitchen with a particular attention.

She has been nominated Ambassador for Expo 2015.

THE RECIPE

MULTI-SHAPED PASTA WITH SEAFOOD AND 'CACIO & PEPE'

PASTA MISTA, BRODO DI PESCE CON CACIO E PEPE

FOR 4 PERSON

160 g Mischiato Forte
Pastificio dei Campi
8 red tomatoes fillets
1 teaspoon fish sauce
4 mussels
4 clams
4 white shrimp
4 red shrimp
8 barnacles
40 g white fish diced
4 asparagus
powder parsley
Espellette pepper powder
4 tablespoons pecorino romano
8 tablespoons of vegetable broth
500 g bisque
4 dulse seaweed leaves
8 peppercorns sarawak
2 tablespoons chili oil

Boil a pot of salted water and pour the pasta and cook for 4 minutes. In a pan, boil the bisque and pour the drained pasta and continue to cook. Briefly sauté the red prawns, barnacles and heat through the white fish. Season the white shrimp with Evo oil and salt. In a glass blender pour the hot broth and add the cheese and blend until you get a fairly thick cream. Cut the toasted pepper grains and crush into pieces large enough with the help of a mortar. In a plate place the pasta finished with a little of the chilli oil, all the ingredients as desired and finish with Espellette and parsley powder.

PER 4 PERSONE

160 g Mischiato Forte
Pastificio dei Campi
8 filetti di pomodori ramati
1 cucchiaino di fish sauce
4 cozze
4 vongole
4 gamberi rossi
8 gamberi bianchi
8 percebes
40 g pesce bianco tagliato a cubetti
4 asparagi
polvere prezzemolo
polvere peperone d'espellette
4 cucchiai di pecorino romano
8 cucchiai di brodo vegetale
500 g bisque
4 foglie di alga dulse
8 grani di pepe di sarawak
2 cucchiai di olio al peperoncino

Portate ad ebollizione una pentola di acqua salata e versateci la pasta cuocendola per 4 minuti. In una padella portate ad ebollizione la bisque e versateci la pasta scolata e continuate a cucinare risottandola. Da parte saltate brevemente i gamberi rossi, riscaldate i Percebes e il pesce bianco, condite i gamberi bianchi con olio e sale. In un bicchiere da minipimer versate il brodo caldissimo e aggiungete il pecorino e frullate fino ad ottenere una crema abbastanza densa. Tostate il pepe e riducetelo in pezzi abbastanza grandi con l'aiuto di un mortaio. In un piatto componete la pasta lucidata con l'olio al peperoncino, tutti gli ingredienti come desiderate e finite con le polveri di prezzemolo ed Espellette.

ACKNOWLEDGMENTS

We are most grateful to our colleagues in Open House Worldwide organization who enthusiastically participated in this publication. Many thanks to all the architects, writers, journalists and chefs who donated their time and their professionalism to Taste of a City project. And of course, our gratitude to Susan Berardo for her creativity, efficiency and cooperation.

The team of Open City Roma

All photos and text are granted by the organizations involved in this publication. All rights are reserved and Open City Roma responds only for the materials it has specifically produced.

Titolo | Taste of a city

ISBN | 978-88-91197-15-3

© Tutti i diritti riservati all'Autore
Nessuna parte di questo libro può essere riprodotta senza il preventivo assenso dell'Autore.

Youcanprint Self-Publishing
Via Roma, 73 - 73039 Tricase (LE) - Italy
www.youcanprint.it
info@youcanprint.it
Facebook: facebook.com/youcanprint.it
Twitter: twitter.com/youcanprintit

Finito di stampare nel mese di Luglio 2015
per conto di Youcanprint *Self - Publishing*